# Energized

# and

# Engaged

How to be The One Everybody Wants to Work With.

# Peter G. Albini

To my wife, for putting up with the process of completing this book.

To my parents:
Mom, for giving me the skill of communication and Dad, for the gift of storytelling.

# Table of Contents

## Opening Thoughts
The Tools..................................................................6

## Chapter One
Being the Best..........................................................9

## Chapter Two
The Dime Man........................................................13

## Chapter Three
What is Work Ethic?..............................................18

## Chapter Four
Communication......................................................21

## Chapter Five
Networking.............................................................26

## Chapter Six
Team Work.............................................................30

## Chapter Seven
Enthusiasm.............................................................36

## Chapter Eight
Critical Thinking....................................................42

## Chapter Nine
Professionalism……………………………………………..48

## Chapter Ten
Share Holder…………………………………………….....57

## Chapter Eleven
Stake Holder……………………………………………....60

## Chapter Twelve
Who is the Customer?......................................................64

## Chapter Thirteen
Satisfied Customers……………………………………….68

## Chapter Fourteen
Repeat Customers……………………………………......77

## Chapter Fifteen
On the Clock……………………………………………...88

## Chapter Sixteen
Your Family is Depending on You…………………….97

## Chapter Seventeen
Save Your Company Money…………………………….104

## Chapter Eighteen
Who Gets to Stay and Who Has to Go?............................108

**Chapter Nineteen**

Education at Home………………………...………………114

**Chapter Twenty**

Education at School……………………………………...118

**Chapter Twenty-One**

Education on The Job……………………………………..123

**Chapter Twenty-Two**

What Drives You?..............................................................127

**Chapter Twenty-Three**

Where Do We Go From Here?...........................................135

# Opening Thoughts

## The Tools

Every company, organization and/or operation has a few people that seem to be the ones that everybody wants to work with. Those people are the ones that make it past rounds of lay-offs. They are the ones that are considered "Irreplaceable".

> You will get out of it only as much as you put into the whole concept.

Although no one person is irreplaceable, you can work towards making yourself so valuable that others are replaced before you.

I am of the opinion that wise people have the ability to learn from the lessons others have learned the hard way. It is my intention, to help you become the one everybody wants to work with, by sharing with you in the following pages what I have learned and will include some of how I learned it. It is my intent to deliver to you lessons and principals you can apply to your life.

This book will give you the added advantage of learning lessons without the time our aggravation of learning them the hard way.

There are sections for you to add your thoughts regarding the points I'm making. The purpose of the book is to help you become the best you can be; to help you become "The One" people want to work with.

Like any other tool, it will only be as good as the person holding it. You will get out of it only as much as you put into the whole concept.

# Chapter One

## Being the Best

> Are you willing to put your name on the work that you do?

The best way to be the one everybody wants to work with you should start with a strong work ethic. One of the ways to define work ethic is to look at the quote from Dr. Martin Luther King Jr.

> *If a man is called to be a street sweeper, he should sweep streets even as a Michelangelo painted, or Beethoven composed music or Shakespeare wrote poetry. He should sweep streets so well that all the hosts of heaven and earth will pause to say, 'Here lived a great street sweeper who did his job well."*
>
> *Martin Luther King Jr.*

That quotation by Martin Luther King Jr. was embodied by Ed Mahoney, the man that taught me work ethic. Ed, defines work ethic as, "Getting up in the morning and doing what needs to be done to take care of your family. To do the job that you agreed to do and to do it well".

For me it is a matter of pride. Are you willing to put your name on the work that you do? It may be my artistic nature, but I liken it to an artist that will sign their work, they do that for two reasons. One is that they are proud of the work they have done. The other reason is that they want the world to know who did it.

After working on a project or task, stand back and look at what you have done. Are you proud of the work you have done? Are you willing to tell the world, "That's my work"? Are you proud to put your name on the work you have just completed?

As mentioned I learned work ethic from Ed Mahoney. When I started putting this project together I interviewed him. As we started talking about work ethic, he said to me, "Do you want to know where it came from? Of course my answer was yes. He proceeded to tell me the story of the dime man.

# Chapter Two

## The Dime Man

Ed Mahoney was a small boy at the end of World War Two. The transition from a war time economy to a civilian economy was hard on the country. The economic situation that most families found themselves in was that of living from hand to mouth, or paycheck to paycheck.

> From then on it became his desire to work for the things in life that he wanted.

It was during that time that the older boys in the neighborhood told Ed that not only could you ask for stuff from your neighbors on Halloween, but for Thanksgiving as well, this was a good thing, in his young eyes. At 4 years old he had already figured out that free stuff was good.

Being a cute kid, people responded to him. Ed set up a network of freebies. Among them he had his jelly doughnut lady and the dime man.

For the jelly doughnut lady it would work like this. He would call up to the jelly doughnut lady's window, "Do you have any jelly doughnuts?" If she did she would put one or two in a bag and drop them down to Ed.

Sitting on the stoop in the Bronx, he would ask this particular man that walked past him, "Got a dime, mister". The dime man would reach into his pocket and toss him a dime.

His winter and spring was full of jelly doughnuts and dimes.

All of this changed one day when he was on the stoop with his father and the dime man walked by. Just like every other time, Ed called out, "Got a dime mister?" The man dug out a dime and sent it through the air. Ed pocketed his new dime.

His father asked, "What is that about?" Not waiting for an answer, he continued. "You know people work hard for their money. They should not give it to you unless you give them something of value in return".

For a young boy the words of his father made a lasting impression in his approach. From then on it became his desire to work for the things in life that he wanted.

As a hungry kid from a poor family in the Bronx, he set himself up to have the things he wanted. Ed set up a new network.

At the age of four, Ed would sort bottles for the local market. His pay was a large sandwich that would take this small boy most of the day to eat. After he was done with the bottle sorting, he would walk over to the soda bottling company and sweep their sidewalk. His pay there… a soda.

With his "Pay" he would get on the subway and enjoy the ride to the end of the line and back. His only worry, would be getting home before supper.

This "operation" set into motion the desire to work for what you want, and to enjoy the rewards of hard work.

Every one of us has a "Dime man" of one sort or another. We all get money from somewhere. It may be a boss at a traditional company. You may be self-employed so your "Dime man" is your customer. Regardless of who the "Dime Man" is. You are left with one question. Are you giving the "Dime Man" something of worth?

# Chapter Three

## What is Work Ethic?

When I started this project, I started with the thought if I want to be the one that everybody wants to work with, I would need a strong work ethic. That thought lead me to a more focused question: "What is work ethic?"

> There is a major skill set that make up a concept we describe as work ethic.

As I asked the people around me we all seemed to have the same reaction that work ethic is somewhat like a kiss. You struggle to define it and describing it is even harder, but you do know when you have it.

Upon further research, I have found a report that set out to describe the concept of work ethic*.

In that report, there is an overarching view that there is a major skillset that make up a concept we describe as work ethic. Those skills include;

communication, networking, enthusiasm, teamwork, critical thinking and professionalism.

To help you become "The One" I have filtered those concepts through my life experience and I have expanded on those six major skill sets.

# Chapter Four

Communication

I have met people that decided that communication was not their strongest skill. Armed with that information they have picked a career that they thought would fit in with their skills. What could be so hard about going into accounting?

In accounting you only have to deal with numbers. Numbers are numbers and they are the same even across language barriers. What these people have found out is that they have to interact with their co-workers, bosses and

> Sending information that is not received or not understood is not communication, it is just talking.

most importantly, they have to interact with the person or organization whose money they are working with. Even math related occupations have communication needs.

Communication is a two way street. This involves a level of give and take. Being good with communication eases the way for others to want to work with you. If they struggle to communicate with you they will be less likely to want to work with you.

I once heard a story from a retired Navy communications officer. He was sharing with us his position on the concept of good communication. The story goes like this.

> *If one of my radio operators would have come to me and said message sent sir! I would have thrown him overboard. Sending a message means nothing. The correct thing to say would be message sent and received, sir!*

Sending information that is not received or not understood is not communication, it is just talking.

In the work place there are many opportunities to communicate; not only with the paying customer but with your co-workers as well. The sharing of duties must be communicated so everybody understands their role in the task or project. Communication is also key in explaining why you did what you did, especially if it is not what was in the original scope of your task.

This has happened to me a number of times with mixed results, but I will stand by my use of communication when justifying my actions. Many times I would start with, you asked me to do X. This would show them that I did listen to what they asked me to do. I was doing it and noticed that 1, 2 & 3 were not accounted for.

Showing that I not only know about my job, I care enough to make sure we all are doing the best we can for the sake of the project. "And so I ended up doing A, B & C". The person I am handing my work to now has the best information that I can deliver.

Do the people you work with and for know why you do the things you do? Do they understand that you know and care about your job? If they don't, then maybe you need to work on developing the line of communication. Take the lead by demonstrating the skills to communicate that information to them.

This flow of information is after all exactly what communication is all about. It is through the communication skill that you can show others your professionalism, enthusiasm and critical thinking skills. Showing them that working with you is beneficial to them and the company as a whole.

# Chapter Five

Networking.

I'm not in multi-level marketing. Why would I need to network? These are good questions.

> When your co-workers have their basic needs met, they are more pleasant to work with.

We all bring different assets to the things we do. Working is no different than any of the social settings we are involved in. The people and companies that you have worked with in the past are not exactly the same as the rest of your co-workers. Each one may have better contacts then the ones the company has "Been using for years".

The collective skills and knowledge are truly greater than the individual parts. The network of people is also better for the organization when you pool all the contacts of each person involved.

The engineering company I worked for need another draftsman. Through the networking process I was able to bring in an employee. This new employee ended up being one of our better hires. He was fast becoming a rising star. It would not be long before his name would end up on the letterhead.

He ended up being such a star that our company could not hold him. It was from the network of a lower level employees that the company had a rising star.

Besides the business aspects, there is a social component to the workplace. Your networking skills may bring just what is needed for a co-worker to meet a non-work related need. When your co-workers have their basic needs met, they are more pleasant to work with. It is almost a self-preservation tactic. Using your networking skills you can create a situation where everybody would want to work with you because you have the skills and knowledge to help them and are willing to offer that help.

Keep the networks open and share them with your organization. You will both benefit.

Networking is also a fantastic way to show off your teamwork skills.

# Chapter Six

Team Work.

If we each had a nickel for every time we hear "There is no I in team". But it is a truism that cannot be ignored. This is a lesson we try to teach our kids by putting them in organized sports.

With the advent of "project teams" in business, we find that team work is become more important than ever.

> Each one of those members has their own life experiences...

In a non-project team environment, you could hand work off to somebody and let them just sit and grind it out. With the project team environment workload is shared and that creates an environment where teamwork becomes more important.

When it comes time to put together a project team, it is critical to be the one everybody wants to work with.

Each member of a project team now has their work dependent on others. Each part is a part of the whole.

Working with teams can be challenging, but if done with a willingness to work together it can be an effective way to operate.

Understanding that each team has individual members, and each one of those members has their own life experiences and communications styles. Matching personalities with tasks makes for a smoother team experience. The member of your team that works best with numbers should not be the one who has to stand and give reports on a regular bases. How well do your skills fit in with project teams? Are you giving people the opportunity to use their gifts and skills for the good of the team?

There are some who, no matter how your work with them, will not fulfill their team duties. There will also be members who will work to take over the entire project. Working with these and finding tasks that will meet their needs while still achieving what is still for the good of the team, will be a challenge.

The key to meeting that challenge it to sell the idea of "whose name is on the door". All workers are brought in for one reason. That reason is to do their part for the good of the company. If they fail at that one overarching goal, then the door may be their next stop.

This concept is not limited to projects and client satisfaction. I remember learning somewhere along the way a story on why Japan was beating the United States in the quality and business environments. I will briefly summarize it for you now.

*Every employee in the factories of Japan has a task. It is a sense of national pride that they do a good job at their task. However there are no limits to who can and should do a job. If the president of the factory is walking through a room and the floor needs sweeping, he will pick up a broom and sweep the floor.*

Do you implement this philosophy in your work environment or company? This played out one day at my office. We had a defrosting refrigerator leak water all over the floor in the break room. I grabbed a mop, and in my tie and dress pants, I was moping the floor. One of my supervisors walked by and said, "You know we have a guy to do that."

I thought back to the story about Japan, and smiled. He may have heard the same story so my response was not met with protest. I said, "It needed to be done, and I am standing right here".

Yes, we did have a guy to do that sort of thing, but as a part of the team, why would I even think about uttering the words, "That's not my job"? How does it make you feel to hear "that's not my job"? You might not have said them, but have you thought them?

To function well in the team environment, you should be able to tap into your teamwork skills as well as the other necessary skills. Those skills include, but are not limited to communication, networking, enthusiasm and critical thinking.

# Chapter Seven

Enthusiasm

Enthusiasm. Many people believe that the words "enthusiasm" and "work" do not go together.

The hard fact is that enthusiasm is one of the keys to a good work ethic.

Many people lack enthusiasm and are unhappy with the work they do. They head to work on Monday morning with dread and stress.

> Are you doing all you can to show your enthusiasm about being there?

A startling fact that I have heard, but not verified is that many people have their first major heart attack on Monday morning. The attitude they have about the work they do is making them sick. If this is true then is basically proves my statement that there is disconnect between enthusiasm and work. If people had enthusiasm when heading to work they would not refer to work as one of those four letter words.

There is an old adage that goes like this: if you do what you enjoy, you will enjoy what you do.

I agree. It is my opinion that there is no shame in the value of working hard, but *unwanted* hard labor should be reserved for criminals.

Picking a career should be done when you understand your own personality and emotional needs. People who are fixers by nature should not go into law enforcement. They will see things that they cannot fix and it will start to eat them alive.

This is a good opportunity for you to learn from the hard lesson of enthusiasm one of my co-workers lived out.

I had a co-worker that did not bring enthusiasm to work. He was a draftsman, but cutting grass at a golf course would have made him much happier. In his case the money was not an object, so his staying in a job he hated seemed odd. His discontent was evident when he would be given a task that he thought was not enough work or a bit too hard for his desired level of effort, he would physically throw the work back and say "I'm not going to do that!" did I mention that I *HAD* a co-worker that did not bring enthusiasm to work. This was a guy that nobody wanted to work with and it was evident throughout the company.

The enthusiasm for your line of work is important. You would hate to have people you have worked with tell a similar story. Referring to you as the one that they HAD as a co-worker. Wouldn't it be far better for you to be the one that everybody wants to work with?

Revisiting Ed Mahoney, my work ethic mentor, here is a man that was born with a birth defect that almost killed him. He could have just lived off of disability and not worked. He had that burning desire and enthusiasm to work and provide for his family.

As he tried to find job at the ship yards, they would give him a physical to see if he was physically able to perform the job he was applying for. Each time they would look at his back and see the 2 inch hole at the base of his spin and ask what happened. Explaining his condition at birth, the physical would end right there and he would not get the job.

After repeated attempts it came down to an employer final giving him a chance. He was so enthusiastic about the opportunity to work and provide for his family that he made a vow that he kept through his entire career. If an employer is willing to give me a job, I will not blame them if I get hurt on that job.

His enthusiasm for work got him in the door. His hard work, enthusiasm, professionalism and critical thinking is what helped him stay in the industry for decades.

You worked hard at getting "in the door" at where you are working. Are you doing all you can to show your enthusiasm about being there?

# Chapter Eight

Critical Thinking.

Murphy was right. Anything that can go wrong will go wrong. Now what?

> Your approach with critical thinking could impress others around you.

I worked with a retired Marine. He was well known around our office for telling everybody,

*There are no problems… only solutions waiting to happen.*

He believed that if you applied critical thinking to your situation, you would find your solution.

We both had the same philosophy that there is an unacceptable answer when facing a challenge and that answer is:

*"That's the way we have always done it"*.

Critical thinking is looking at a situation, knowing where you want to go. Then finding the path to get there.

With an open mind and a willingness to learn new things or even to fail in the first few attempts to find that path. You have an opportunity to be an innovator in your industry. You have the opportunity to be the star or hero of the project. You have the opportunity to be the one that everybody wants to work with.

These opportunities are available to those who look at situations and apply critical thinking. It is not just the innovation, but the ability to make decisions in a timely manner. Knowing that you have made them quickly and they are the right decisions.

For all the computer programmers out there, it is looking at the big picture and understanding the

"If/Then" scenarios. If we do this, then that will happen. Can we live with the "then"?

Critical thinking is the steering wheel for driving your organization. It is not just management that has their hands on the critical thinking wheel. It flows all the way down to line workers.

Here are some life lessons about critical thinking in the workplace. My mentor Ed told me about critical thinking in his career. He looked at every job that he worked on as a big puzzle. To him the entire plumbing structure was just a big puzzle. He would spend time thinking about what pieces needed to be where so the whole thing would come together.

One job in particular, he amassed a plan to have all of the supplies delivered to each house in the tract. The three bathroom lot would have three toilets, the two bathroom plans would have two toilets delivered to that lot.

The first day or two was verifying that all the parts and pieces were where they needed to be. As each lot was prepared to receive the plumbing, he and his team would assemble the puzzle in one day. A house a day.

Ed would approach each and every job with his critical thinking skills in full effect.

His approach has managed to trickle down to me. When facing a task that looks like it might be too big for one person to handle in an allotted time. I step back, look at what has to be done. Then I formulate a plan of attack.

How do you approach large tasks? Are they overwhelming or do you see them as a challenge?

Do you form a game plan? Do you accept the challenge as a chance to shine?

The skill of critical thinking, like all others is refined and improved upon through practice and use. As you continue to practices your critical thinking skills, you may find that people want to work with you because you are able to find answers when others are stuck in a box.

The next time you are faced with a challenge, think of it as an opportunity to work on your critical thinking skills. You might end up looking more professional. Your approach with critical thinking could impress others around you. Inspiring them to want to work with you again and again.

# Chapter Nine

Professionalism

Many people associate the term being a professional with getting paid. There is a component to that argument.

> Are you applying your skills to be the one management trusts as a top professional?

The concept of professionalism is much deeper than that.

A scene in the movie, "Ferris Bueller's Day Off", the trio drop of a car in a parking garage. The attend tries to put Ferris' nervous side-kick at ease by saying "Trust me I'm a professional".

When you hear that statement does that statement put you at ease? If you said that statement to the people you work for and with, would they be put at ease?

There are some hard and fast realities that can define professionalism. One of those is the getting paid for what you do. There is also a "Feeling and emotional" quality about the term professionalism.

Since this is a book about a concepts, and the rules for each industry are different, I will stick with the emotional side of the discussion.

Your level of detail and attention is a component of this skill. To me it all comes down to actions and attitude towards your endeavor that instill the trust of others. The attitude that make others want to work with you.

Others would like to trust that if they give you a task, assignment, or job that it will be done on time and correctly. They want to rest assured that you will understand the pitfalls that can occur and will plan to avoid them.

They also need to trust that you understand and will comply with the regulations, rules and laws that govern the task or assignment that you are undertaking.

To achieve a level of professionalism that will proceed you, it involves action on your part. These actions include, but are not limited to; increasing your education, showing up and demonstrating your skills and talents. A willingness to learn as your occupation/endeavor changes.

I had the "pleasure" to experience an event where a line workers understanding of professionalism was not operational. This would be a good time to learn from the mistakes of others.

I was at a professional baseball game. I love the peanuts. The "Peanut guy" was coming by and I bought a bag. As I was eating them I could taste the slight hint of cigarette. I kept eating them and not sure where this taste was coming from.

As I reached into the bag I pulled out a dry roasted and salted cigarette-butt. It had been broken off and the paper was folded over the remaining tobacco. How could this happen?

There was a line worker in a peanut processing plant that did not take his or her professionalism seriously. As a "Professional" peanut processor, the question, "If I throw a cigarette butt into the process then what will happen"? Should not even come to mind. Unfortunately for me and the peanut company, it did.

The next year there was a different brand of peanuts sold at the same stadium. You have to wonder, was it the lack of professionalism by one line worker that cost an entire peanut company a major league baseball stadium contract?

The peanut story was how NOT to do things. Here is a little "how to" for you to save time and learn from the lessons others learned through time and hard work.

Things never stay the same, they are either growing or dying. When they are dying, it is time to learn ways to ride to the end or find a new occupation/endeavor.

If they are growing, it is important for you to remain competitive, that you learn and understand the new processes, procedures and requirements.

Here is an example of how professionalism was evident in my career.

In the construction industry the final step is for the design team to take the contractors field notes, the notes on how they actually built the project, and create a set of drawings that reflect the actual filed conditions. The term is known as "AS-Built" drawings.

This take a bit of skill and understanding of not only the drafting and design trades but also an interpretation of the contractor's intent of the notes and comments submitted.

Combining those notes is a difficult and time consuming process, with a set of requirements that is different than other things done in the design side of construction. This is a task that will only be trusted to the top professional available. Are you applying your skills to be the one management trusts as a top professional?

This was a task that landed on my desk more than any other co-worker, simply because I demonstrated the critical thinking required to interpret the contractor note and the enthusiasm to apply my professional skills for the betterment of the company. Accepting the fact that I may not be shareholder of my company, but I am a stakeholder. If the company does well, they will stay in business and I will still be the one that everybody wants to work with.

We have covered the basics of what work ethic is and how it can help you be the one everybody wants to work with.

What is your definition of the term "Work ethic?

# Chapter Ten

Share Holder

As we journey through this discussion of how to be the one everybody wants to work with, in addition to the skill set that makes up work ethic, there are two terms that should be defined. The definition of these terms will help clarify what other want, need and expect. Those terms are "Shareholder" and "Stakeholder".

> Every kid that has ever set up a "Lemon-aid stand" has received a lesson in the definition of a shareholder.

Shareholders are the people that put money into a venture with the expectation that that venture will be successful and provide a return on the investment. These are people that are willing to take risks and deserve to be rewarded for their risk taking.

They are not heartless, they just know the value of the money they are putting into a venture. They also are people that believe in the venture enough to put their money behind it. Without shareholders no business will get off the ground.

The shareholder concept is not limited to big business and Wall Street. The small time guy who will scrimp and save to buy a pushcart vending opportunity is as much a shareholder as the venture capitalist that throws millions of dollars behind a large business.

Every kid that has ever set up a "Lemon-aid stand" has received a lesson in the definition of a shareholder. They buy or pick the lemons, squeeze the juice, paint the sign and then put time in, keeping an eye on the operation so it is not taken over by a neighbor kid. They receive an education on the concept of the time and effort invested, is worth the potential profits.

# Chapter Eleven

## Stake Holder

Shareholders are the ones that put money behind an idea or operation. They are not the only ones that have a stake in the success of an operation. All of the people that find themselves needing the good or service provided as well as all of those who provide that good or service are considered stake holders.

> When the operation is running and running well, all of the stakeholders can get their needs met.

Customers that need the product are willing to pay for it because the need is there. They will do what is needed to meet the needs they have. That is the stake they have in the operation.

The shareholders are also stake holders, they have a financial stake in the success of the operation.

Sometimes things aren't about others, they are about you. You are a stakeholder in whatever company or organization you are involved in. The worker bee's the ones that make the wheels go around have a different stake then the customer. The good or service will meet the need of the "Customer" the need that the workers have is the need for a paycheck. Where do you fit into the stakeholder spectrum?

Shareholder can provide the money and in some cases provide some of the skill and knowledge that is needed to make a company run. But they cannot do everything. They are willing to pay "Employees" for the skills and knowledge that they bring to the operation.

All of the stakeholders have one common goal. That goal it to keep the operation running. When the operation is running and running well, all of the stakeholders can get their needs met. The

"Customer" gets the good or service that they are looking for. The shareholder gets a return on their investment. The hands on deck that produce the goods and services that are needed, also get their needs met; they get the paycheck. In a well run operation all parties involved will be getting their needs met.

# Chapter Twelve

## Who is the Customer?

To start the discussion about customer satisfaction we must first address the question, "Who is the customer?"

Your customer is not necessarily the person or company that pays for the service that you or your company provides. That is the easy answer and is not as accurate as one might believe.

> How many times are you serving the customer in the work flow that you are involved in?

The role of customer is a moving target. It transfers as fast as the work flow that you are involved in. The true definition of a customer is as follows:

> *The person that receives your work when you are done with it.*

Some examples for this concept are as follows:

In the engineering work flow, a designer comes up with a concept. The designer will pass it along to the draftsman. In that portion of the work flow the draftsman is the customer receiving work from the engineer. After that draftsman completes the work with the information provided, it is then sent back to the engineer for further design.

The engineer is now the customer, receiving the work provided by the draftsman. After some back and forth between these two customers, the work is finalized and sent to the client. The client that has contracted with the engineering firm is the final customer. It is at this time that the perceived customer finally gets the work.

In a restaurant environment the customer flow starts with the wait-staff. They take an order and then pass their task on to the cooks in the kitchen.

The cooks are now driving the work flow, and the wait-staff becomes the customer receiving the work that the cooks have finished. From there the wait-staff checks for accuracy and final presentation then delivers their work to the person that walked into the restaurant as a "Customer".

How many times are you the customer in the work flow that you are involved in? How many times are you serving the customer in the work flow that you are involved in?

# Chapter Thirteen

Satisfied Customers

After defining who the customer is we need to look at what the customer wants and what we want from them. They want to be satisfied and we want them to return. We want the coveted "Repeat customer" and the only way to get them, is to have them satisfied.

Continuing to look at both sides of the "how to" lessons in the book, here are both a how NOT to do it and a how TO do it stories.

> How well are you treating your customers?

First the "How NOT" to do customer satisfaction. This is another lesson that you do not have to learn the hard way.

The joy of home ownership brings about many opportunities. One of them is to fix things when they break. A wise homeowner will fix what they can and bring in professionals for the things they cannot fix.

I can do a lot with wood, but electricity and water are two things that have perplexed me over the years. When I have plumbing problems I am quick to pick up the phone. Picking up a wrench will only result in a bigger bill when I finally give up and call in the professionals.

On this particular day one of our toilets needed "some work". Being a good homeowner I called. I scheduled for a plumber to come in and deal with my issue.

The dispatcher/scheduler gave me a 4 hour window on when I would see a plumber. At the end of the 4 hours, I called and was rescheduled with another window of time. The day my plumbing event started had now ended with no plumber showing up to my house.

I called another plumbing company and we started the same dance. The good news on this whole experience was that we had more than one toilet and only one was out of commission.

At 10 o'clock that night, the second plumber still was a no-show. The most amazing thing happened. The phone rang, it was the first plumbing company asking if I still needed another plumber.

This event got me thinking about customers and customer service. The things I started thinking about were who is the customer and how should they be treated in a successful operation. How well are you treating your customers?

What are your thoughts?

_____

_____

_____

This story had a happy ending. A friend of ours, who we had not seen in a few weeks showed back up. And of all things, he was a plumber. He fixed our problem and did it at a good price.

The two plumbing companies missed the mark on satisfied customers. The final result is that they not only missed the opportunity to both have me as a customer and the idea of me becoming a repeat customer was also lost.

And now for the "How to" example.

For every story about bad customer service there are good ones. I will now share with you an experience where the worker in his operation had a great understanding of customer satisfaction and what it can do for the stakeholder and shareholder alike.

Fast food restaurants are the epicenter of service base business. The level of service has, in my view, been sacrificed for the speed required to put the "fast" in the fast food title.

One day I had made a regular stop at a fairly busy McDonalds. The crowd was restless the employees were frantic. I placed my order. This was a busy time and the orders were faster that the cooking.

Not all of the food required to fill my order was prepared. The gentleman behind the counter put one of the two burgers I ordered on a tray. We waited about five minutes for the second batch of burgers and fries to be cooked. The tray was shaping up to be one order of hot French fries, one hot burger and one sort of warm burger.

If you were behind the counter in this situation what would you have done? Among the options you would have had was to complete the order as fast as possible and move on to the next customer.

Your thoughts:

_____
_____
_____
_____
_____
_____
_____
_____

I truly expected the order to be completed as fast as possible with one warm and one hot burger. What I encounter was an employee that decided that customer service was important and food temperature was equally as important.

The gentleman took the burger that had been sitting and replaced it with two fresh burgers and the order of hot fries.

The level of customer service was appreciated so much that I walked out of that restaurant picked up the phone and called the 800 customer service number. Not to complain about the speed of the service, or the crowd of people, but to complement the young man that chose customer service over the cost of a wasted burger.

It has been over 20 years since that event, and I still think about it every time I drive by that particular McDonalds and when I think, speak, or write about customer service. In addition to telling that story often, I will still spend my money at that particular McDonalds.

Your thoughts

_____
_____
_____
_____
_____
_____
_____
_____

# Chapter Fourteen

## Repeat Customers

As discussed earlier, there are two types of customers. Internal and external. The internal customer is the co-worker that receives your work when you are finished with it. The external customer is the one that engages your company for a good or service. Regardless of which customer we are referring to, repeat customers are important. Your effort in keeping both types of customers happy will go a long way in making sure you are the one that everybody wants to work with.

> I was learning the value of returning customers, and how important they are for the success of any business.

I had the opportunity to learn this lesson first hand. Let me share with you that lesson.

As an employee of Chuck E. Cheese I had the opportunity to meet some fascinating and interesting people. Some of the regular customers fell into those categories.

Mimi was a mentally disadvantaged young lady. She would come in with her family every other week. Mimi loved Chuck E. Cheese, the only stuffed animal that would hug back.

When they did arrive Mimi made sure that I knew it. Mimi would seek out Chuck E. Cheese and from the time they arrived to the time her dad said it was time to go home, Mimi would be by the side of Chuck E. Cheese.

The job of Chuck E. Cheese was to be there for all of the families that came into spend their time and money to be fed and entertained.

With one little girl wanting to dominate the time of Chuck E. Cheese, what would you do if you were in the costume? Would you drop her off at her parents table? Would you ask one of the other employees to explain to the family that Chuck E. needs to spend time with the other customers? Those were options available.

Your thoughts:

_____
_____
_____
_____
_____
_____
_____
_____

I know what I did. I was learning the value of returning customers, and how important they are for the success of any business.

In my attempt to be the best Chuck E. Cheese I could be, I figured out the schedule and would position myself so I could see what was happening in most of the restaurant, but could keep an eye on the door.

When Mimi's family hit the door, Mimi leading the way, dressed in her Sunday best dress with the Patten leather shoes. It was like a romance movie, we would both head towards each other in a full run. We would meet in an embrace and then I would have a side-kick for the rest of the evening.

The ground work for a lesson in repeat customers was being laid and management wanted me on the clock to keep the customer happy. They wanted to work with me.

Every other week Mimi's family would come into the same store and do business, this was a win-win situation. The family got entertainment and a meal, Mimi got to hang out with her friend Chuck E. Cheese and the corporate offices made a profit on the night.

What would you do?

_____

_____

_____

_____

If Chuck E. Cheese did not care about the job he was doing, that family would not come back. They may have spent $150-200 in one visit. Even if the spend less and they come back twice a month they will keep the operation running.

Getting customers in the door is hard; why not have the ones you already served as repeat customers? It is much easier than trying to keep an operation running on first time customers.

With repeating external customers your company will stay in business. This makes both the shareholder and stake holder happy. This is not to discount the importance of repeat customers of the internal variety.

Internal customers that decide not to repeat can only result in two things. The first being that you will find yourself bouncing from department to department within the company. When you move from department to department you can find that you are behind and always trying to learn how to fit into the new dynamic that you find yourself.

The second result is a bit more devastating. You could find yourself out of the company altogether. Since this is a book on how to be the one everybody wants to work with, let's fix that potential problem before it becomes a reality.

Working to have satisfied internal customer helps your desire to be the one everybody wants to work with. If you are satisfying people's needs they will want to keep dealing with you.

It comes down to a simple equation. Repeat customers equals repeat pay. Your effort in that equation determines your level of success. Some of the skills that would help in your quest for repeat customers would be professionalism, critical thinking and enthusiasm. One of the best ways to have repeat customers it to have satisfied customers.

The idea of 100% customer satisfaction is truly important for your success, regardless of which customer you are serving. How do you achieve satisfied customers? Here is how I did it when I learned the lesson about satisfied customer.

Here is some background for the story and the lesson learned. I have heard the baseball and church should be canceled on account of rain. When you work in a kid based restaurant you can add one more thing to that list.

On a cold rainy night, parents are not big on loading up the kids and driving them to a restaurant that will wind them up more, just to take them back home.

This creates an issue for management. Do they cut the staff down to minimum for the night or do they offer all they can to the much smaller number of customers?

On this cold and rainy night, the restaurant was empty except one family in the room with the automated lion that sang Elvis songs.

What would you do in that situation? Some of the options available would be to hang out with your co-workers. Ask management to let you go early?

It is always good to catch up with the people that you work with. There are always better things to do than hang around a restaurant on a rainy night. Besides management would love to save the money by not paying you for entertaining one family.

Your thoughts:

_____
_____
_____
_____
_____
_____
_____

I was on the clock, so I spent my time in the King Room. This family got the personal attention that many are seeking when they go out to a restaurant. The little girl in this family was not only entertained, she was worn out.

With the attention they received the family stayed longer then they may have otherwise. The little girl and I danced; the parents bought pizza, beer, sodas and kept putting tokens into the lion.

The amount of money they spent more than covered the cost of me being there on the clock. Not only did they help fund the operation, this family left with a positive impression of our restaurant and are more likely to come back in the future.

Satisfied customers are the driving force in a restaurant lasting more than 12 months.

# Chapter Fifteen

## On the Clock

In your quest to become the one everybody wants to work with, it comes down to it one big question is; who is the most important "Everyone"? In the work equation, the most important one is the one with hire/fire authority. Management has thoughts and opinions on what is expected from you.

Can I have your undivided attention? The days of trading time for money are over. For management to decide that you are the one they

> When you are on company time your actions are directed by the boss, the tasks, and the customers.

want to work with, you must have an understanding of the terms "Company time" and "Personal time", there is a difference between the two. On personal time you are free to do whatever you want. Sounds like a great deal. The only problem is most of the things people want to do takes money. In order to get that money, you need to spend time on "Company time".

On "Company time" your options of what to do are limited.

Working at a pizza restaurant that has an arcade is not all fun and games. There are times when the business of the restaurant takes precedence. These are the times when management decides who they want to work with.

On one spring evening in 1984 I was doing the business of running a business. In a restaurant dishes need to be done and napkin holders need to be stuffed. This is a reality regardless of what is happening in the outside world. Every four years the world however seems to slow down to a spectator sport.

When the Olympics happened in 1984, they happened to be in my home state. We, like many others in the United States would be offered a chance to see the Olympic torch as it was run throughout this country.

On the night it went by my place of employment, I was tasked with napkin duty in the main dining room. I was working my way down a row of tables dragging the big tray of napkins and I noticed that it was real quiet. To quiet for a restaurant that caters to kids and families.

I looked up and found that I was almost alone. The last co-worker said the torch was coming by. I had a decision to make. What would you do in that situation? You could walk out and see it with everybody else. You could clock out and hope you did not miss it as you made your pit-stop at the time clock.

What would you do?

_____
_____
_____
_____

The thought that ran through my mind was that I get paid to do a job. I decided I would do the job that management expected me to do.

After about a half an hour, one of my co-workers came running up to me asking, "Did you see it?" I looked and pointed at the row of tables holding stuffed napkin holders and said, "I am on the clock".

Proud of the decision I made, I felt I would get another chance to see the torch, it was clear to me that being a good employee was just as important as the Olympics.

The reply I received from him, could have been in a foreign language. He shook his head at my choice and with wide eyes and a bit of national pride in his voice he said, "It was worth getting fired for".

On a side note, when that torch was run into the Los Angeles Coliseum and lit the Olympic flame for the games that year, the television was on and the crowd was gathered around.

I am not sure what the scene looked like from the side, but there stood Chuck E. Cheese with the rest of the customers watching this event that was happening 40 miles away from where we stood and was shown on televisions around the world.

That was not my last encounter with company time and the Olympic torch. 16 years after I made the decision to be an employee rather than a spectator, the Olympic torch was heading through the town that I was living in at the time.

I had a different job and different experiences that had shaped my life over those years.

Early Sunday morning the torch would be run within a mile from my house. As a teenager I made the decision I am still proud of, understanding that I would one day get another chance to see the Olympic torch. The time had now come.

My time to see the Olympic torch also overlapped with the scheduled work for my second job. I was once again faced with the same decision. Do I go to work or do I justify my absence with the story about missing this event as a teenager? What would you do in the situation?

Your thoughts:

_____

_____

_____

_____

_____

_____


I went to work that morning. I am still proud of the decision I made, both in '84 and '00. However, after two near misses. I have a plan for the next time the Olympic torch is run through the United States.

My plan is to at the very least, schedule a day off from work. The master plan is to arrange for a chance to run a leg of the torch relay. After two near misses, I think I have earned the right to that honor. There are not many things in life that I believe I am owed or entitled to, but after two misses, a chance at the Olympic torch is one of them.

When you are on company time your actions are directed by the boss, the tasks, and the customers. Your customers and/or employer are paying you for your skills and talents. Give them the best you have; give them your undivided attention. The results will show in your product. When your product is top of its class, your pay and more importantly your reputation at work will follow. People will find that with your dedication you are the one they would like to work with.

# Chapter Sixteen

Your Family is Depending on You.

Are you the bread winner in your house? As the head of your house. Even you the single readers are in charge of running your household. The line of stakeholders is deep. You becoming the one people want to work with is important, so you can keep on supporting yourself and your family.

> I found that he was driven to make sure we, as a family, did not know the hunger that he knew as a kid.

Living under the same roof as Ed Mahoney, I had the opportunity to learn a great deal about work ethic and doing whatever it takes to work.

There was one overarching lesson that was learned, not as a sit down lesson to be taught, but by observing his action.

After years of living and acquiring my own experiences regarding work ethic and walking through the same roles as father and husband. I was able to talk with him about that lesson and the factors that drove him to do what he did. We talked about his lessons taught.by example.

Work ethic and the desire to be the best, was so ingrained in this man that when I brought the subject up, he had no idea what job I was talking about. After you read the story you would think that a job like that would stick in a person's memory.

The story is this.

Construction work comes in waves. There are boom years and lean years. The hope is that you make enough in the boom years to cover the expense of the lean years.

With six kids to feed and clothe, work was necessary even in the lean years of construction.

During this particular time, there was only one job at the union hall that was available. The job was a sewer tie-in.

To save you from the details I will only say the two tools needed for this job were a shovel and hip-waders. Would you take a job like that?

Your thoughts:
_____
_____
_____
_____
_____
_____
_____

Ed took that job. He would drive 40 miles each way, offering a service for a paycheck. That service was something that not many would provide, but Ed did it to feed his family.

I learned a lesson when he was working that job. Here was a man that would get up at dark O'clock, drive 40 miles, shovel sewage for a shift then drive the 40 miles to get home and shower it all off.

The thing that stuck out the most was that he would joke about the job he was working. He had a positive attitude about what many would consider a "Crap" job.

When we talked about it 25 years later, he did not remember that particular job. However in the time I spent with him I found that he was driven to make sure we, as a family, did not know the hunger that he knew as a kid.

The lessons taught from Ed's sewer tie-in job, made an impression even without me knowing it.

In high school I found that I needed a second job. The job that came available to me was that of janitor. I found that dealing with the drama of high school was not as important as my need to work.

I took the job and I found that I was now getting paid to clean toilets and it did not matter what my peers had to say about the line of work I was in. knowing that I could and would be a janitor was helpful in my future. How far are you willing to go to meet your needs?

In trade school I needed a job, because I found that I was addicted to the concept of eating at least one meal a day. The school would help students find work. The job that came available was that of janitor.

Once again I was getting paid to clean toilets. I knew my entire working career would not be what I was doing while in school. Providing for myself was more important than what other people thought of me. Once again revisit the Martin

Luther King Jr. quote that we started with. We can interpret it to read "There is nobility in cleaning toilets".

I found that I had learned a lesson in how I perceived some of the more menial occupations. By working as a janitor, I have found that it is a noble profession. Would you clean toilets in the manner of the greats like Michelangelo, Beethoven Shakespeare?

Another lesson I learned about myself was with the right enthusiasm, I will take and then perform well, at any job that provides me with the opportunity to provide for myself and my family.

In approaching your occupation with the same enthusiasm will help you become the one everybody wants to work with.

# Chapter Seventeen

Save Your Company Money.

Life is expensive. Rent/mortgage, car, health and auto insurance, food, utilities; it all adds up.

Despite what some might tell you there is no free lunch or car payment, rent, phone bill…. You get the picture. In your quest to provide these things for yourself and your family, you find that they all have a value. To pay for them you need to have the funds they require. Once those bills start, they never stop.

> The days of trading time for money are gone and will not be coming back.

It may seem like there is a never ending stream of bills, so you need a stream of income that meets or exceeds those bills. Where do you think those streams of income come from?

I can tell you that after a number of years meeting those expenses, the money needed comes from employment. Getting a job is the easy part.

Once you have a job, you start trading service for money. The level of money you will receive is dependent on the level of service you provide. You may be a nice person, but you need to be a productive nice person for a company to continue the service for money relationship. The days of trading time for money are gone and will not be coming back.

Most companies don't really care if your level of income starts to decline. Their expenses and profit margins are non-negotiable. The shareholders and stake holders are in the game and they all also have the same expenses that you have. Why should they give up meeting their expenses so you can have things for free? You would not give up your

"Stuff" to give other people things for free that you have to work for.

The whole thing is dependent on the service for money equation. Your part in that equation is fully determined by your level of engagement.

# Chapter Eighteen

## Who Gets to Stay and Who Has to Go?

Business runs in cycles, the economy also runs in cycles. As employees or employers, there needs to be a level of preparedness to deal with those cycles.

> Now came the decision that no boss wants to make.

Once again looking at the idea of trading service for money, or as Ed's father told him so many years ago, "You need to give people something of value before they give you money."

Companies have employees that bring a great deal of service and some that do just enough. You know who they are and you know the term we have for those people. Yes, they are dead weight.

Like any other thing that needs momentum to achieve progress, dead weight will slow it down. During my time managing a department for an engineering firm, I had to deal with a bit of dead weight.

A surprising lesson on deadweight, for me came not during the lean times, but during a time of great boom. We seemed to have more work than we could finish in a timely manner. I recognize that we had a few employees that were slowing the process down.

I wanted to get rid of them and bring in others that would be less of a drag on the department. A few of us were in the 60-70 hour a week range and others hardly made 38 hours in a week. We needed help not dead weight. When I had enough, I went to the boss.

He listened to my position then said something that made me more frustrated than when I walked into his office. He said to me "Half a hand on deck is better than no hand on deck".

While it is true if we had to get the work done with just the guys that were putting in the effort. The extra 38 hours of work each week put in by the dead weight would have extended us to the breaking point. We did use those hand on deck.

Then what happens many times and people seem to forget, it came time for a down turn in our business. Now came the decision that no boss wants to make. They had to find answers to the question, who gets to stay and who has to move on?

The guys in the trenches can answer that question a bit better than the guy in the upstairs or corner office. It is the guys in the trenches that have heard and know the real answer to the old joke: How many people work at your office? About half of them.

When the work slows down the dead weight is the first to go. Who is the deadweight? It is the people that do not exhibit the six skills that make up work ethic. They are not enthusiastic, critical thinkers. They do not show professionalism. Networking and teamwork are not part of how they operate in the workplace. And they are not well versed in communication with others.

Employers are willing to keep and occasionally "carry" an employee that exhibits the work ethic skills. They are interested in keeping good employees. Employers are interested in saving the money associated with training new employees when they once again need all "Hands on deck".

Some will stay and some will go. Are you doing all you can to stay? Are you one of the few that can be called "Deadweight"? The future is in your hands. You can make changes that are needed to keep your job. You hold in your hands the roadmap to be the one that gets to stay. You hold in your hands the opportunity to be the one everybody wants to work with.

# Chapter Nineteen

## Education at Home

Lessons are all around you. It is up to you to learn from them. They have been around you since the beginning. Some of them have been obvious. Other may have been a bit more subtle. The lesson about not touching a hot stove was taught to you is some way. For my son it was the hard way before I could stop him. At less than a year old he touched the hot stove. He cried and has NEVER touched a hot stove again. Lesson learned. The lessons about work ethic may have been the ones that were taught with a more subtle approach.

> This approach has helped me in overcoming the "Valuable Negative Information approach" of learning life's lessons.

In your case the lesson may have been a negative approach. The things you had seen and experienced were not the things that would help you in your future success. The way we learn from those lessons can be summed up in the statement: I learned how NOT to do it.

If that is your situation you now have the opportunity to learn with the positive approach. I had a lot of life lessons taught to me with the negative approach. The success I was able to find in those lessons, was that I was able to look at what I saw growing up and do the opposite. This approach has helped me in overcoming the "Valuable Negative Information approach" of learning life's lessons.

It has been my experience that parents and guardians do the best they can with what they have. To learn the lessons about work ethic and life in general at home I recommend that you take the good and apply it. Take the negative and do it differently with the goal of reaching a different outcome.

There are people out there that put so much effort into NOT working that if they put half as much effort into finding and keeping a job they would become successful. There are others that work so hard that they forget the important things in life. The challenge we all face is finding the balance, to make us good employees and good people in general. Those lessons start at home.

# Chapter Twenty

## Education at School

There is a thought process out there that is "All I ever needed to know I learned in kindergarten". There is a bit of truth to the thought. When you first start school, in kindergarten, you start learning social skills that will carry with you for the rest of your life. Among the things that you learned in kindergarten are communication skills, team work, critical thinking and enthusiasm. Do these skills sound familiar? They should, we have covered them in the "What is work ethic" section.

Communication. Early in our formal education we start learning how to express what we want and need in a manner that will get us what we are looking for. We

> Yes all we ever needed to know we learned in kindergarten. But the lessons did not stop there.

learn how to listen to instruction and to others around us. These are skills that will be applied to a strong work ethic later in life.

Teamwork; it is when we are in kindergarten that we are formally taught how to play together. We start learning the lessons of teamwork that will help us understand all of the people we will have to interact with over the course of our lifetime. Including but not limited to co-workers and employers.

Critical thinking; lessons on something as simple as stacking blocks starts the ground work for critical thinking skills. How high and in what order can we stack without having the whole thing come tumbling down? We start processing the skills needed to answer the "If/Then" questions of life.

Enthusiasm; can be translated into attitude, and in what kindergarten class are you allowed to have a bad attitude? Yes all we ever needed to know we learned in kindergarten, but the lessons did not stop there.

In high school the personalities got bigger. The problems more dramatic, and the work a bit more challenging. The first lessons in time management started to creep into the daily planning that you had to do. Another one of the lessons that help form a strong work ethic.

After high school, college is the final proving ground before "Real Life" is college. That is where you will put to use all of the skills you learned along the way. Many employers are not so concerned about the subject you have a degree in, as they are concerned with your ability to handle the pressure of college life and your ability to prioritize and mange time.

Sometimes we miss the point of formal education. I am just as guilty as the next guy when we have all said, "When in the real word will I need to diagram a sentence?" or "Will I really need to find this math answer in the real world?"

The truth is, it was never about the math answer. It was about my ability to look at a problem and find a way to answer it. Our ability to solve problems will be needed throughout the rest of our lives. The answer to "*x=?*" will not stop or start the world turning.

Education at school is so much more than what the teacher puts on the board, or the publishing company prints in text books. It is the life lessons learned along the way that will help you create and maintain a strong work ethic.

# Chapter Twenty-One

## Education on The Job

On the job training. This was a perk or enticement used to get candidates in to jobs. With an opened mind it can also be the tool you use to make yourself the best candidate for the jobs you are applying for.

> Each job we have along the way will lay the ground work for the success on our next job.

I support the thought that everybody should work some sort of job as part of their high school experience.

For some of us it started earlier than high school. I had the good fortune to grow up in a time where a young boy could be a paper boy. (This is one of those lessons that you learn from somebody else that I mentioned in the opening of this book).

At the age of thirteen I was basically running a small business. A franchise if you will. I would come home from school and there would be a stack of newspapers on my porch. I would have to prepare them for delivery, then make sure they made it to the customers in a timely manner.

At the end of the month, if I wanted to get paid for my efforts I would have to go to each customer and ask them to pay for the service I have been providing. As I would stand face to face with my customers, they would tell me about my service (good or bad) as they were paying for it.

My desire to have those as positive conversation, drove me to provide the good service. I learned about customer service, accounting, and time management.

Each job we have along the way will lay the ground work for success on our next job. Why would you not want to get a head start on that learning curve? The sooner you start, the farther ahead of the competition you will be.

Many of the work ethic lessons I learned and want to share with you, I learned on my first two jobs. Those lessons helped propel me to the positions I have been able to attain in life. These lessons can help you become a success in all you wish to do.

# Chapter Twenty-Two

## What Drives You?

There are things that drive us to be the best at what we do, for my mentor Ed it was the Dime Man and his father's reaction. The lesson that drive me, was a young girl I met on my first job at Chuck E. Cheese. What drives you? If you have not found that one motivating event in your life, you are welcome to learn from mine. It is my goal to share my life experience to help you become the one everybody wants to work with.

> That was a lesson that has inspires this book, a lesson that can help make you the one that everybody wants to work with.

The event that drives me is this.

Working at Chuck E. Cheese I encountered many different types of people. Kids that knew no fear and would break away from their parents to be with Chuck E. Parents that would avoid Chuck E. (must be the ones that are also afraid of clowns).

I had to learn how to deal with the kids that loved Chuck E., but had smaller siblings that were afraid of the rat.

One late Saturday afternoon, a dad came in with his two kids. The boy was about 7 and full of energy and enthusiasm. His sister was more around 11 and quite.

The boy was all over Chuck E. Cheese. After a physical and aggressive greeting from the boy, I reached out for his sister to shake her hand. She hid behind her dad, this was an odd occurrence. An 11 year old kid is not usually afraid of a costume character.

What would you do in that situation? Some of the choices I had in that situation included but are not limited to: keeping your distance from the whole family, spending time with the boy, letting the girl do her own thing.

What would you do in this situation?

_____
_____
_____
_____
_____
_____
_____
_____

Understanding that a five foot six inch tall rat can be intimidating, I did what I always did in that situation. I squatted down, spread open my arms in a welcoming gesture. The dad said something that I will never forget, "It's okay honey, he's not a doctor or a nurse".

This changed that whole game. This girl was not afraid of a tall rat, she was afraid of "any stranger". Her experience was that strangers would be a part of the trauma that she was going through.

Armed with this new information, you now have other choices. You could keep your distance from the whole family; this poor girl is already going through enough. Spend time with just the boy, his sister has more than likely been the focus of the family. Let the girl do her own thing, kids can find their own fun at Chuck E. Cheese without the help of a costume character.

What would you do with this new information?

_____
_____
_____
_____
_____
_____
_____

I made it my mission that night to get this girl to love Chuck E. Cheese. I pulled out all the stops. Rules be damned, I was going to get this girl to "Love" Chuck E. Cheese.

I would beat on this girl's father. Wave through windows. Run by toying with her brother. I even when so far as to run by, pick up her brother run him through the kitchen, drop him off next to his sister. The boy laughing all the way.

Two hours of using every trick in the book, and a few that are against the rules, it was time for this family to leave. As they headed to the door, Chuck E. Cheese was with them. Boy's hand in one hand, the girl's hand in the other.

As we all made it to the door, I decided another rule was going to be broken. I walked them to their car. When we reached the car the boy bounced on in. The girl quietly got in and put on her seatbelt.

Their dad closed the door and shook my hand. What he had to say to me changed my life.

His words contained such emotion and gratitude, "Thank you. She has cancer and 6 months to live. You really made her night".

I was 17 years old, and I cried as I walked back to my post in that restaurant. It was that night in that parking lot that I learned the most important lesson about customer satisfaction and work ethic as a whole. That was a lesson that has inspires this book, a lesson that can help make you the one that everybody wants to work with.

The lesson learned that night was, no matter what you do for a living, no how insignificant you think it is, do it to the best of your ability. You never know whose life you will effect.

# Chapter Twenty-Three

## Where Do We Go From Here?

Nothing in life, worth having is free. Most things that you want will require some work. The world, and all that is available, is yours for the taking. The only question is, how hard are you willing to work to get what you want?

If you want the best, and who doesn't? Give the best you can, at work, and you will be rewarded. The rewards may not be of the monetary kind. Some you those rewards will be lessons and stature that will carry you to bigger and better things in life. Another reward for giving your best is that you can become the one that everybody wants to work with.

> Give the best you can, at work, and you will be rewarded.

The good news is the secondary benefits are that some of those rewards will be of the monetary kind.

It all comes down to the level of effort you put into it. Work ethic is not something you just wake up with one day. To obtain it is a long and drawn out process. It is my hope that this book has been a roadmap for you to chart your own course towards the things you want in life.

Having a strong work ethic will move you past the people that do just enough to get by. You have an opportunity to stand head and shoulders above the rest.

Work ethic is a tool. A tool is only good if the person holding it knows what to do with it. A hammer won't drive a nail unless you swing it at a nail and hit the nail. Work ethic takes effort. More than just effort it takes focused effort. With that focused effort you can be the one everybody wants to work with and you can have it all.

Notes:

*THE CENTER FOR WORK ETHIC DEVELOPMENT

White Paper: Whose job is it anyway? Strategies for Increasing Job Retention

December, 2012

www.workethic.org

## Peter G. Albini

Motivational speaker, Author and Master of Ceremonies.

To Book, contact at:
(714) 287-0600
petergalbini@gmail.com

You can also visit his web site:
www.petergalbini.com

www.ingramcontent.com/pod-product-compliance
Lightning Source LLC
Chambersburg PA
CBHW051711170526
45167CB00002B/626